IN
GOD'S
HANDS

BY
SUNSHINE

I Am Gods Daughter

When GOD speaks, I listen! Obedience is a must in The Kingdom of HEAVEN! God has placed this in my spirit as a witness of HIS mighty works.

We sometimes think God has left us during the worst parts of our lives, but really, HE is right there beside us or even carrying us through the most difficult times.

Here are some of my testimonies of how amazing God has been in my life. Through the good, bad, ugly, sad, and joyous times. God has always been there.

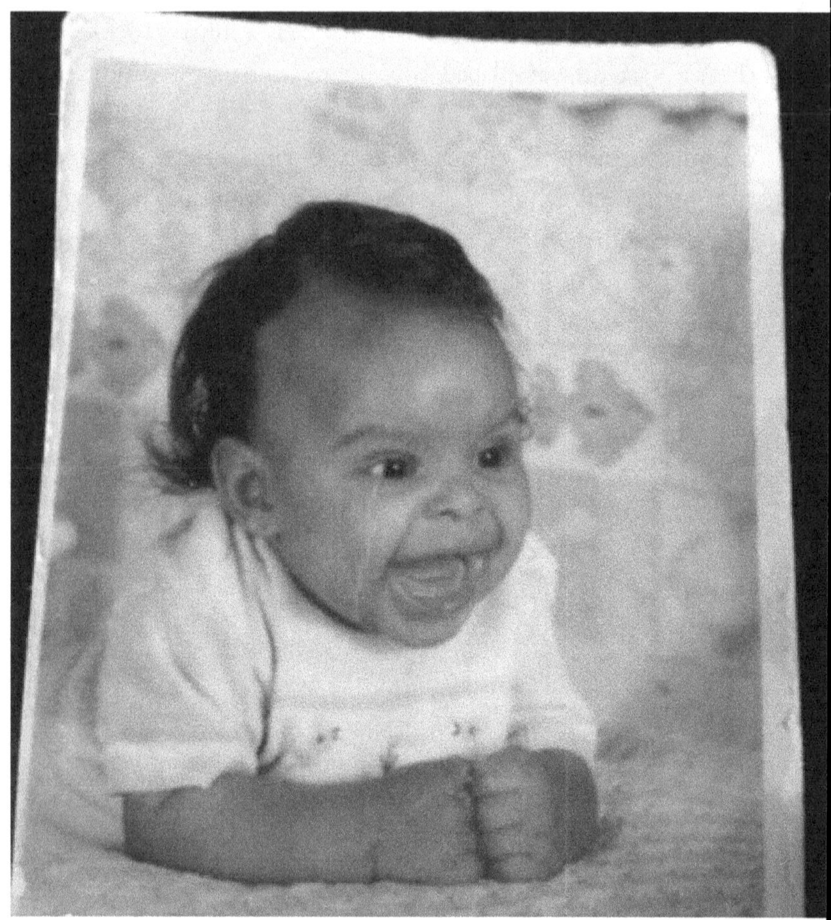

During the labor my mother told me that she was having complications, so the doctor had to perform an emergency cesarean (c-section). I was a chunky baby weighing 8 pounds 8 ounces. Due to my mother's pelvis being too small for me to travel naturally through the pelvis. Here is where the delivery takes a turn. My mother has not turned 18 yet so she needed a parent to sign for the c-section. Unfortunately, my Grandmother Hazel was nowhere to be found. My biological father was at the hospital with his mother/my grandmother Inez. My grandmother Inez signed the forms, so the doctors could perform the cesarean (c-section).

FAMILY BEACH OUTING

When summer hit, our family stayed at the beach all day til it started to get dark. That is how much we love the beach. The water has always been a place of serenity for me ever since I was little. I find my most inspiring/creativity while I am near the water. (Water = Holy Spirit).

On this hot summer day, we always packed a cooler with hot dogs, hamburgers, cold cuts, drinks (soda, water, juices, and daddy's beer). The car would be packed with two Queen-size sheets, big umbrella, two lounge chairs, towels, change of clothes for the nighttime, radio, extra batteries in case the radio dies, charcoal, volleyball set up, cards, reading books and our pails. Summertime in our family was a lot of great times outdoors.

We would either go to Jones Beach or Robert Moses. These beaches were the favorite go to beaches on Long Island, New York. Now if you have never been to these beaches, let me warn you about these waves. The waves at Jones Beach & Robert Moses are strong and if you're not careful, you can lose your life.

So, on this hot summer day, we chose Robert Moses beach to stay the day there. We arrive at the beach and start unloading the vehicle. Everything is finally out of the vehicle but now we must transport everything I named to a nice spot on the beach. Everyone loaded their arms and shoulders with items to lessen the back-and-forth trip to the car. Whew the hot sun, burning sand on our feet, but it was so worth it. The set up took a few minutes as always, but now we are all settled down to stay for the entire day at the beach.

We all loved the beach. Daddy Roy was ready to hit the water. Adriane and I were right behind him. Setting up the area in that hot sun, now we needed to cool off. The first entry of the water is always the coldest. For me to enter the water I will let my feet get used to the water, then walk further in and let my legs get used to the water and then the rest of my body. I know that's a long process but that is how I do it still to this day. My father was different, he would just jump right in and dunk himself a few times under the water.

Once we are all in, let the games begin. We would have fun in the water just swimming around and playing games (Marco polo). Daddy would have a shiny object for us to find in the water sometimes. Daddy would drop the item and then we had to dive and retrieve it the item. Dag, I miss those family fun times, and I miss daddy.

Mommy started making us our sandwiches because she knew we would be hungry when we got out of the water. Now I will stay in the water until my lips turned blue and shivering. That's when daddy would force us out of the water. We would eat and then either play a game, take turns singing songs, play volleyball or read a book. Once our food was digested, our parents would allow us to go back in the water.

Adriane and I sprinted back into the water ready to have more fun. Now the time is close to 5:00 p.m. so the tide is now coming in strong. The waves are so strong at this time of the hour. This is when the undercurrent is more dangerous for anyone. Being kids, I think I was 10 years old, and Adriane was 7 years old. Daddy was coming also to swim with us. One thing about our parents, they were very protective of us. Adriane and I were swimming and not paying attention to the waves at this time. The waves started coming fast and hard towards us. As kids laughing and joking around not thinking anything was wrong, we stayed in that area still laughing and swimming.

One wave came and knocked us back a little, so we said okay it is time to move closer to the shore. We heard our father calling us to hurry up. My sister started swimming closer to shore and so did I but then another wave came, and this time pulled me under. As I was trying to get up from being pulled under another wave was coming simultaneously (Now in swimming class the teacher always said don't panic.) Keep your breathing under control and swim with the water and not against it. So that was what I thought I was doing. So many waves kept coming and now I did start to panic. All I heard while under the water "I GOT YOU"! The next thing I knew a hand reached down and grabbed me. It was my father pulling me up and taking me to shore. I was coughing uncontrollably and spit up a lot of water. The nervousness in my parents' eyes showed me they were so concerned. I stayed out the water for the rest of that day. **(But that voice wasn't my fathers I heard… at the time I didn't know Gods voice at that age. As I write this, I now know it was GOD**.) Think about it, I was underwater, and my father couldn't see me, so how did he find me and pull me out? GOD nothing but GOD!

<u>WATCH OUT</u>

I am now thirteen years old, which means I can finally walk to my friends houses or to the store without any restrictions from my mother. My mother was overprotective of me and my sister (**looking back now I don't blame her**). It's Saturday early afternoon and I asked to go to my friend Linda's house who lived right up the street near 8th Avenue. Linda and I have been best friends since elementary school. My mother and her mother were friends as well when they were in school together.

So, I was walking on the right side of West 11th Street that had a sidewalk. My two cousins Andre and Torrey were on the opposite side of the street. We spoke while walking in the same direction, when out of nowhere a Bronco truck jumped the curb and now was heading towards me. In that split second both my cousins screamed out towards me "**WATCH OUT**"!!! I jumped out of the way and into the bushes that was on my right side. I was a little scratched up, but I was safe because of them. They saved my life that day! My cousins were at the right place at the right time. They ran across the street to help me up and made sure I was okay. I was so shaken up and shaking all over. They walked me to Linda's house, but no one was home. So, I continued to walk to 9th Avenue and went to Ms. Vanessa's house. I asked Ms. Vanessa to use her phone so I could call my mother. I told her what happened, and I was too scared to walk home because my nerves were shot. My mother came right away to pick me up. I cried so hard that day. But God

If God did not place my cousins at that point of time and on that street with me, I would have been killed. That truck was speeding and did not even stop. That was GOD protecting me!

Mother Hiller (Pastor/Great Aunt)

<u>MOTHER HILLER</u>

This amazing Woman of God was my Great Aunt and my Grandmother Hazel sister. She helped raise the entire community in Huntington, New York. God's love blessed her to live a long prosperous life. A street has now been named after her! She did great works throughout her life.

Every Sunday growing up as a child, we would go to church. Mother Hiller would preach her sermons and then afterwards our family would meet at her house for Sunday dinners. Mother Hiller house was on a hill near Huntington train station. The adults would send all the children downstairs to the basement to play, while the grownups would prepare dinner for us. We had a lot of fun down in the basement. Our boy cousins would teach the girls how to protect ourselves and showed us some fighting techniques. My other cousins would watch television until it was time to eat. I would sometimes sneak out and go upstairs to the kitchen and sit with the elders. I learned so much from them. Sitting with the elders I learned: how to cook, family history, collected memories, true meaning of fellowship and family values. Precious memories embedded in my memory.

Mother Hiller received her wings on May 18, 2006, just three days after her birthday. She was a sharpshooter and stood her ground. She played a pivotal role in all our lives. She is greatly missed daily.

Sunday mornings at Mount Calvary Church

she is carried
by His grace,
fearless in His
strength, and
empowered
by His love.

I Am SHE....

GOD'S TIMING

—

IS PERFECT.

<u>HEAD ON COLLISION</u>

It was sometime in 1997, I forgot the exact date, but I had my first car accident. Currently, I was living in Richmond, Virginia. I remember the day like it was yesterday. I was driving a bronze Mitsubishi Gallant four door vehicle. In the vehicle was: Precious, Moët (my fur baby) and myself. Ej was 8 months old, so I left him home with his father. The road I was traveling on was a windy one lane going both directions.

Precious was sitting in the front passenger seat and Moët was in the back seat enjoying the ride like always. (Moët would always ride with me anywhere). As I proceeded down the windy street, all I saw was a white Jeep Cherokee heading toward me at a fast speed. The male drive lost control of the vehicle. The vehicle was coming straight towards my vehicle. In Virginia let me explain the streets to you, on both sides of the road there were ditches and it would have been worse for both of us if we were pushed off the road.

I started praying and placed my arm in front of Precious to try and hold her back from getting seriously hurt. (**Back in that year the vehicles did not have airbags**). The next thing I know I'm hearing the fire department trying to wake me up and get us out of the vehicle. The fire department had to use the jaws of life to get me out. The jeep hit me head on and the rest of the vehicle slid into my driver's side door. When I finally woke up, I was in a daze, and it took me a few moments to realize what happened. Moët flew up to the front seat and he was sitting on Precious lap. Moët was licking me to try and wake me up. Then I tried to turn but my body was in so much pain. By this time the police officer and fire fighter were telling me don't move. The firefighter introduced himself to me and told me the next steps they are about to take to get me out of the vehicle. The Firemen began to use the jaws of life tools on my vehicle. The reason they had to use the Jaws Of Life on my vehicle: The roof caved in on me; the driver's door was jammed; the hood was pushed to the windshield and the seat belt was jammed. The fire department kept speaking with me to try and calm me down but now I was freaking out.

The steering wheel caved in on my right knee, the brake pedal smashed into my right foot, my head had a fat knot on it (**Hematoma**), my right hand was swollen, had a cut on my right pinky, my head was in major pain, neck was hurting, and my back was on fire. The fire department finally retrieved me out of the vehicle and the ambulance/paramedics went into full action mode. The paramedics checked my vitals, put a neck collar around me and then slowly placed me on a back board. Moët was not allowing them to take me without him. Moët was my protector and I had to keep reassuring him that mommy was ok. I remember seeing the guy who hit us on the ground handcuffed. I asked why he is handcuffed to the paramedics. The paramedics told me that the other driver's blood alcohol levels were twice over the limit. The police officer stated he was now under arrest. The anger that formed in my body at that time was unexplainable. The paramedics said the way the impact hit us; we should not have survived. But God! God had his hands upon us. Yes, we did get injured, but we did not die! Again, another miracle. We survived because of God. Nothing BUT GOD! Thank you, LORD!

<u>CLOSE THE DOOR</u>

EJ was in his walker at my mother's house. This little boy loved that walker and terrorizing the dogs with it. So, one day my mother went downstairs to the basement to check on something and Ej's father also went down to help her, but he forgot to close the basement door. I was in the laundry room and heard my mother scream Nikki. I darted so fast out of the laundry room to find my mother carrying EJ upstairs in his walker. I flipped out trying to figure out how he got down the stairs. My mother and his father said he left the door open but what they said next blew our minds. Both stated when they heard the walker, they ran towards the basement steps and saw EJ being guided down the stairs, meaning some angels were carrying his walker down the stairs so he did not have any injuries! Look at God dispatching Angels to protect my baby. They both said they would not have believed anyone if they did not witness this with their own eyes.

Another Miracle God has done for me and my family. My baby could have died that day if it wasn't for the Blood of Jesus and HIS covering!

<u>HIS VOICE</u>

Myles is now six months old and it's time for him to be Blessed (**By a Priest**). I've been looking for a church home that my family can attend permanently, but every church we visited just didn't feed my spirit. Being raised in a church with great teachings spiritually and a built foundation, I was not getting it from any churches that we attended. February 2011 that's when everything changed for me. I asked my desk partner at work about her church and if her husband could bless Myles. I spoke to the Pastor who is now currently my Pastor. Pastor stated the church did have a slot open to have Myles blessed on the 4th Sunday in February. I spoke to Myles's father and suggested we visit the church a week early just to make sure the Pastor was a true Man of God/Shepard of the House. Listen not anyone can just touch or speak a word over my children. Remember I am assigned as their mother to watch, pray, fight and guide them properly. I must cover and protect my three heartbeats and their gifts.

As I enter First Calvary Missionary Baptist Church and opened the sanctuary doors, I heard GOD say, **"Welcome Home".** Right then and there I said this is our church. The children and their father looked at me strangely and said we had not heard him preach yet. I said I do not need to hear him preach because GOD already put his stamp on this house. Now anyone who was not brought up in the House of God would look at me or anyone strangely. I get that but I am looking and seeking GOD! Now GOD has answered me right away before the sermon even began. Service started and the worship set the atmosphere and then the word that Pastor preached was confirmation. I wanted to join right then and there but their father said wait one more visit to see before joining. Now their father did not grow up in church so I understood but told him next week I will not wait for him to join. I said when GOD speaks, I listen.

I will admit my gifts were dormant for years because the enemy scared me. No one in the family explained the true meaning of the gifts that our family carries. Now I am at First Calvary Missionary Baptist

Church. My gifts are activated. This time with the Pastors help, I was able to learn about my gifts and how to sharpen the tools to access all of them fully. Once my gifts were activated all hell broke loose in my life. God did warn me the more Intune I became with my gifts the more the enemy will attack. Whew the weight of the mantles my family carries I had no clue till I was in my early 30's. God started out slow with me and the training began.

I now have a personal relationship with GOD/ABBA/YAHWEH, and I love it. Do I love attacks? **NO, I DO NOT LIKE ATTACKS, NOT AT ALL** but it comes with the Mantles. Many of my family members have let their mantles fall, transit to Glory or just gave them up. Not me I know what my calling God has for me, and I will not let GOD down. I do not mind letting man or woman down but not GOD. GOD has brought me a mighty long way and I refuse to let him down. GOD and I have a personal relationship and I will be obedient, and I will always hold myself accountable. I am not perfect only Jesus Christ was. We all fall short, but I own my actions! I can throw my own stone at myself, again I know I am not perfect, but my heart is pure, and I am chasing after Gods own heart.

<u>APPENDIX</u>

I was cooking lunch in the kitchen for my baby Myles who was nearly six months old at the time. While I was preparing his lunch, I received a sharp shooting pain hit me in my body. The pain was so intense it knocked me on my knees literally. The pain was shooting from one side of my stomach to the other side. I started to pray and asked God what was wrong with me. God answered and said Appendix. This was the second time I heard his voice so clearly. After God said that I called my mother right away. I told my mother everything that happened and what God said and my mother said the same thing. My mother advised me to get to the hospital right away because if my appendix erupts and I am not at the hospital all of the toxics can poison my insides and cause me to die. I told my mother that I had to wait for the babysitter to come and then I would head to the hospital. My mother was not happy hearing me telling her that, but a mother has to do what a mother has to do. I was not spending all that money on an ambulance and bringing my baby into a germ filled hospital (Not happening). So the babysitter Ms. Pat showed up and I advised her what was going on. She said she will watch the children until the children's father comes to get them.

So here I go trying to save money and drive myself to the hospital with the shooting pain in my stomach. If I could do it over again, I would call the ambulance right away (can't cry over spilled milk now). Driving to the hospital felt like eternity. The hospital was literally 15 minutes from the house, but I was in so much pain I was speeding, trying to get to the hospital quicker. I arrived at the hospital and parked the vehicle. The walk from the parking lot to the emergency room took even longer because it was so hard to move let alone walk. I finally made it into the hospital emergency room doors and advised the front desk that I have a serious situation and need to be seen by a doctor right away to prevent my appendix from erupting. The woman at the desk had the nerve to ask me: Are you sure you are not having a miscarriage or you may have a UTI. I told the lady I know what God told me and my mother confirmed it. I advised the lady I was not pregnant, and I need to see a doctor as soon as possible. Don't you know those jokers had me in the hospital waiting room for almost an hour. I documented everything and told them if my appendix burst while I am sitting in this waiting room to be called to the back. I advised I will sue and I am a paralegal. After I said that all of a sudden, I am being called to the back for a doctor to examine me. While I wait for the doctor a nurse comes in and asks questions. I advised for the nurse to draw my blood and check the white blood cells count. I advised if my white blood cells are high then it is definitely my appendix. Here goes the nurse asking me was I pregnant and am I sure I am not having a miscarriage. I had to catch myself from snapping at her. I advised the nurse to get the head charge nurse that was working now and have that person come into my cubicle because I needed to be heard. The head charge nurse entered the cubicle and I advised what has taken place. The head charge nurse apologized and took a blood sample from me. Sure enough, my results came back and that is when they got worried and started to wheel me into the operating room. I stopped them and advised that I needed to call my pastor at the time to pray for us before the surgery. Everyone stopped and looked at me. I advised the Shepard of my church will pray over us before they cut me open. I advised I am a prayer warrior and refused to go another step without hearing my pastors voice praying over us all. My pastor answered the phone right away and put his plate of food in the oven, so it stayed warm. He prayed over us all and then I handed my cellphone to someone and off I went into the operating room.

As the medicine was being placed into my veins, the doctor had me start to count from one hundred down and then the lights were out for me. I was knocked out sleeping hard and when I woke up I was in my hospital room near a window.

SIDE NOTE: WHEN I SEEKED GODS GUIDANCE ON WHAT WAS HAPPENING, GOD ANSWERED. THAT IS THE PERSONAL RELATIONSHIP I HAVE WITH MY HEAVENLY DADDY. I THANK GOD FOR MY RELATIONSHIP WITH GOD.

<u>UNCLE RICHIE</u>

A good friend of the family name Richard but we call him Uncle Richie. Uncle Richie has to wear hearing aids due to being almost deaf. One weekend Uncle Richie stopped over to our house and said he was led to see us. He started to speak and fill us in on what was going on with him and his hearing. He advised he has been seeing a specialist and they are willing to try and operate and help correct some issues that he was having with his hearing. Uncle Richie was scared and knew we believed in God so he wanted us to pray. I advised everyone to grab hands and I started to pray. God then told me to break the circle and place both my hands over his ears. God gave me specific instructions and then said to close my eyes and to start praying. After I was done praying Uncle Richies eyes got all big and he said I felt something happen. He then gave me a big hug.

The next month Uncle Richie advised the operation was a success and he said God did it because the specialist said it was a 50/50 chance of being a success or a total failure.

SIDE NOTE: ALLOW GOD TO BE ABLE TO TRUST YOU AND USE YOU FOR HIS GLORY.

<u>WALKING BY FAITH</u>

2015 my walk with GOD increased in a major way. I worked for this insurance company for the past ten years in the claims department. I was so miserable at that company for almost five years but GOD did not give me permission to leave that company until 2015. Through those ten years I would ask God to release me from the insurance company and the answer was always no. Now in 2015 God said you have my permission to leave the job but in my house my spouse at the time did not want me to quit. I told my spouse God has given me permission to leave the job now. My spouse and I did not see eye to eye on me leaving the insurance company. When it came to my gifts my spouse would always disregard them and basically call me liar. So, who am I supposed to listen to you? I want to listen to God but while being obedient to him, I have my spouse at that time flipping out on me and telling me to stay at the company. I am now facing a major dilemma, and I turn to GOD in prayer because God is never an author of confusion. Once I took it to prayer, God stepped in and told me I will follow HIS instructions. The next day after arguing with my spouse I went to work. Still having this heavy issue weighing on my heart, I turned it over to GOD. I worked my regular shift and decided to go get a pedicure after work. While traveling on the main road, a young male was speeding behind me trying to catch the light. The young man did not stop in time and rear ended my vehicle causing rear end damage to the vehicle I was driving. While waiting for the police to come to the accident scene, the pain started shooting through my back and legs right away.

I went to the hospital and the doctor took me out of work due to my injuries. The injuries I sustained during this motor vehicle accident are: two bulging disc, two herniated disc, a pinch nerve, spasms and my sciatic nerve. The pain was excruciating for the first six months. I was assigned to physical therapy, chiropractor and massage therapist. God said to me: I will heal you during this time, but I need you to go back to school and become a paralegal. God said I have an assignment for you, and I know you can handle this. Now I told my spouse what God told me, but he did not believe me again. I told him that I must be obedient to GOD and do what HE has called me to do. Well, that caused a lot of discord in the home. I would go into heavy prayer asking GOD to intercede in my home because I was not having any peace at home with my spouse. GOD said whose report am I going to believe and follow. I told GOD that I am following HIM and I shall walk by FAITH. God told me the places he is about to send me, will bring many to believe in Christ because of my faith. He said do as I say and don't worry about what others say! I'm walking by Faith not by sight!

I signed up to go back to college to become a paralegal. I started college as a full-time student, half on campus and the other half online studies from home. While in college, we opened our home to fostering children per GODS instructions. You heard right; I am in college at the age of 40; getting therapy for my injuries; I am out on medical leave from my job and now a foster mother all at the same time. I was juggling a lot BUT GOD gave the strength during those two years to handle everything all at once. During this time my two youngest sons were watching and rooting for me along the entire way. You can say they saw my journey, struggles and persistence on accomplishing the assignments God gave to me.

When I tell you how GOD moved on my behalf for being obedient, by walking by faith and trusting HIM when I could not see further ahead. God made sure all our bills were paid and nothing got cut off. God said trust him fully and watch what he is about to do. I trusted him even through my pain and heartache. GOD is so amazing and mind blowing. God has not failed me yet. I feel sometimes I failed him and then here God comes sending more blessings my way. I am HIS humble servant. When God says move, I move! When God says speak, I speak! When God says shut up- whew I shut up even when I don't want to.

<u>WINTER STORM</u>

I was working at a law firm in the Town of WIlliamville on Main Street. The weather outside was getting worse by the minute. The snow was coming down heavy, so the office manager Tracey told us to go home and drive safely. As I begin to go down the windy road at a slow speed, I would say I was driving slowly as I could down that windy road. A turn was coming up and I was now applying my brakes for safety when my car slid on the snow and ice, and I lost control of the vehicle. I started screaming Jesus, Jesus, Jesus and then the next thing I knew I felt my car glide down the hill, and I was bracing for impact with the telephone pole I was about to hit. I could not avoid it but when I tell you my car came to a complete stop, and it tapped the telephone pole. First words out of my mouth were thank you GOD for dispatching your angels to protect me.

No damage to my front bumper and I mean not even a scratch. Thank you, God, for your covering and protection.

<u>A VISIT FROM HEAVEN</u>

One glorious night in 2019 a Heavenly angel came to me wearing this beautiful royal blue gown with gold designs on the gown. An angel was faceless, but I knew it was a Heavenly encounter. Just the two of us speaking and enjoying the conversation. The angel told me in the beginning I forgot my assignments but now I am doing everything GOD wants me to do. The angel said to me HEAVEN is proud of me. The conversation was just so enlightening and sweet spirit feeling. That encounter will always stay with me. Then that Sunday after church my Pastor came to me and told me Heaven is paying me attention. I told him I know and then shared my encounter with the angel. My Pastor just smiled.

<u>THE ANOINTING</u>

Sunday, August 26, 2012; Myles was two years old, and he was sleeping on my lap in church at this moment. The choir set the atmosphere and I was praying heavily to the Heavens. I welcomed The Holy Ghost into my life fully. I raised my hands and started to circle my hands in the air slowly and then I just felt God take over my body. I was moving the top part of my body and was moving my arms around in the air and it started out as small circles but then I started to stretch my arms out more and more. Pastor was on the Pulpit and was about to preach but he said I will wait until The Holy Ghost has his way. After service everyone was heading to Darien Lake and a member came to me and said thank you for that anointing you allowed God to do through you. My Pastor and I also talked about what took place in church that day. I told him what it felt like and how honored I was for the Holy Ghost to use me to bless the house that day.

When you ask God to use you and let him! The glory of God's Love, Grace and Mercy. I am so thankful I know God as my Heavenly Father. God keeps blowing my mind.

<u>THE ATTACKS</u>

As I look back on all God has saved me from, the enemy has tried literally to take me out numerous times. I know the plan GOD has for me and my children are great. The enemy has come to me in so many ways but still failed. I refuse to quit because I know who has my back. GOD GOT ME & I KNOW I AM COVERED BY THE BLOOD.

These are just some of my testimonies on how GOD has been with me along the way in my lifetime. When I thought GOD was silent, but HE was still working on my behalf. I am the KINGS DAUGHTER. I am so humble, honored, grateful, in aww of HIS mighty hands.

Allow GOD to use you. Do not think you cannot be used. Be the vessel and make sure you give GOD all the glory.

Have a Pastor or Spiritual Advisor to help guide you with your gifts. Take the proper classes to teach and guide you regarding your gifts. Be very careful who you tell about your gifts. Not everyone will receive you or some will look at you differently. Reveal to those who God says to reveal too and be silent when God says be silent. Trust your instincts always. If something seems off, ask God and wait for his instructions. Trust me, I had to learn the hard way. I spoke too soon sometimes or spoke to the wrong ones who didn't believe my gifts. Many mocked me and even my spouse (he was supposed to be a believer). Always use wisdom and pay close attention. Stay watching and stay praying! We are under attack by the enemy. The enemy wants to silence our gifts/voices/assignments. We must stay diligent and stay always woke!

<u>YOUR ASSIGNMENT</u>

When God gives you an assignment and you must complete it. Some assignments are not easy, trust me I've faced some assignments with a heavy heart, but I still did it. You must be obedient and do exactly what God tell you to do because if not, whew YOU will not have a comfortable sleep until you do. Trust me, I have had many sleepless nights when I was being disobedient.

Remember to do your assignment and then keep it moving. You did what you were supposed to do and that's it. Never add to or subtract to what God tells you to do or say. It's all about God getting the Glory. These are gifts God has given to us and as he had given, he can take right back. Stay in alignment with God. If you fall off the path, dust yourself off and get back in alignment.

Now stop and think of everything that has happened to you in your life. Do you have those BUT GOD moment? Has GOD ever stepped in and made a way out of no way? Has he supplied all your needs? Did your lights stay on when they should have been cut off? Did God save your from dying in that accident? What has GOD done for you or your children?

Now thank him for saving your life.

<u>CLOSING</u>

We are just visiting this world and when our time is up, I want to hear my good and faithful daughter well done. I pray this blesses you. Don't allow anyone to steer you from your gifts! These gifts are given from Heaven, and you should be honored that God created us unique and wonderfully made. God created us in his own image and it's a blessing.

I am going to give you a few assignments now to help you see that God has never left your side as well. Get a pen and start to think of anything that could have killed you. Get ready..... turn the page.

<u>ASSIGNMENT TIME</u>

1. Take a moment and think of your childhood and if anything major happened that could have caused you to die. Write it all down here on this paper.

1. HAS GOD WARNED YOU ABOUT ANY FORM OF DANGER?

1. DID YOU LISTEN TO HIS WARNINGS?

WHAT IS IT THAT YOU ARE SUPPOSED TO DO BUT HAVEN'T DONE IT? GOD WANTS YOU TO GET IN ALIGNMENT WITH HIM. HE WANTS TO BE ABLE TO USE YOU AND MOST OF ALL TRUST YOU. NEVER WAIVER WHEN OTHERS ARE AROUND.

<u>MY PRAY FOR YOU</u>

Father God, I thank you for all you are doing for me and still what's coming ahead. Father, I thank you for everyone who reads this book. I thank you for everyone you send my way. Father allow your will to be done in me and through me as you see fit. Move in a mighty way Holy Ghost! I am just your vessel and I just want to thank you Holy Ghost for having your way.

Father God as I close out this book, I ask that you speak to the ones who read this book and activate their gifts fully and completely. Allow them to be Bold for the Kingdom of Heaven and walk fully in the authority you have given us. This is my prayer in Jesus name Amen.

Essence of God
By
Sunshine

All photos that are in this book, have been taken by Nicole Murphy "Sunshine" and cannot be reused. Nor copywriting of any type from my books.

Essences: love, happiness and peace. Having a special quality or fragrance. Its basic and most important characteristics that gives its individual identity.

Love: an intense feeling of deep affection. A great interest an pleasure in something.

Happiness: an emotional state characterized by feelings of joy, satisfaction, contentment and fulfillment.

Peace: Freedom from disturbance, tranquility.

Father God thank you for allowing my eyes to see past the physical. Father thank you for allowing me to use my hands to reach the people. Thank you for the breath in my body. Thank you for always being there in my time of need as well as my time of joy.

Father thank you for your wonderful creations. Thank you for your wonderful works. Father thank you for speaking in many ways.

Father I am so thankful for you using me as the vessel and how you see fit on using me.

Genesis 1:1
In the beginning GOD created the Heavens and the Earth.
Genesis 1:3
God said "Let there be Light.
Genesis 1: 11
God said "Let the land produce vegetation: seed bearing plants and trees on the land that bear fruit with seed in it, according to their various kinds.

CREATION that was created by the CREATURE!

<u>GODS LOVE</u>

Unconditional love, affection without any limitations or without condition. Completely loves us and wants the best for HIS children.

<u>FOR THE READERS:</u>

Most Heavenly Gracious Father GOD. I want to say thank you before anything else. Thank you for the breath in our bodies. Thank you for the roof over our heads. Thank you for all you keep doing behind the scenes. Father thank you for never giving up on us. Father thank you for your loving kindness. Father thank you.

Father as they begin this book, open their eyes so they can see past the physical and go deeper in the spiritual realm. Father allow, their eyes to start seeing deeper in the spirit.

Father I ask that you open their ears and eyes fully. Father, I ask that you speak in a major way. Father allow, your will to be done in Jesus name AMEN.

In life not everything stays the same. As we grow mentally, physically, and spiritually: we must decide what we want out of life! Who do we want to be when we grow up? Not everything comes so simple to us. Sometimes things change with unforeseen circumstances.

When life throws you a curve ball, stay focus and keep moving forward. Don't get complacent or give up. Take time away from all the chaos or distractions and re-center yourself. You have work to do because others are counting on you and need you.

This book has been created for you to stop and look around you. Embrace your surroundings and enjoy God's creation in the process.

Capture the pure essences of Mother Nature! Capture the precious moments that are taking place right in front of your eyes. Treasure each day because you may never get a second shot.

When was the last time that you just stopped and relaxed fully? Stop thinking about your problems? Stop thinking about work? Stop thinking about everything?

Right now, take a moment and close your eyes. While your eyes are closed, just breath in slowly and then let it out slowly. Do that at least 5 times before opening your eyes. Now look around you with a different pair of eyes. When you step back and relax your mind will align your spirit properly. You are now able to see more clearly of what is right in front of you.

Allow me to show you the beautiful essence of living in the moment. Not allowing your circumstances to dictate how your life should be. God created the Heavens, Moon, Sun, Humans and Earth.

Transition: the process or a period of changing from on state or condition to another. Come with me and look at the beautiful atmosphere. It's the simple things in life that we miss daily.

<u>**Embrace**</u>

Be true to yourself and most of all to GOD. Live your best life and be authentic.

<u>TREE OF LIFE</u>

The beauty of this tree speaks volumes from a distance. Take a moment and just look at this photo and write down everything you can see. Now let me tell you what I see. I see years of history this tree has lived through. The broken branches, the cuts and firmness of the tree. This tree was planted in the heart of traffic. This tree roots are so strong and grounded. God's creation is so amazing. God gives us life in so many ways.

<u>LOOK TO THE SKY</u>

God speaks in so many ways. Are you paying attention? Don't let life pass you by without truly living. Stop and enjoy your surroundings. Take a photo to look back on all the beautiful essences of Gods mighty works.

Presences of GOD

<u>Capture The Moment</u>

Life is precious and everything around us as well.

Take that photo.

Take that Drive.

Take that time to capture the moment, so you can look back and smile.

Life is too short to not enjoy it all.

Embrace life!

Embrace Change!

Embrace Gods beautiful Essence.

<u>Aluminating the Sky</u>

As the day turns to night and the sky illuminates int0 many amazing colors.

Serenity: the state of being calm, peaceful, and untroubled.

GODS CREATURES

God's creation enjoying the atmosphere on a nice warm sunny day in San Diego, CA 2021. Gods' creatures are on one accord peacefully enjoying the day.

Treasure the moment!
Live in the moment!

No matter what happens on your path of life, we will face diversity but stay on the course. God has you covered.

San Diego, California Beach life 2021

<u>AS THE WATER REACHES THE SHORE</u>

Watching the water reach shore and create a splash full of force. Just the little things in life that takes your breath away.

San Diego, California 2021

Marriott Hotel in sunny San Diego, California 2021
Pool side fun

Myrtle Beach, South Carolina October 2021

Looking at this photo I captured on a warm spring evening in Mexico 2019. Breath taking.

Mexico 2019 coral reefs and tropical fish an amazing experience.

<u>RAINBOW</u>

A bridge between the physical and spiritual realm. The rainbow represents the ability to grow spiritually and transcend the earthly realm. God is speaking and when the rainbow appears, just stop and take a moment to enjoy the beauty of it.

Winter 2020
<u>WINTER BREATH</u>

As winter appears the beauty of the snow falling from the sky and landing on the trees.
The pureness of not touched essences of Gods mighty works.
Capture the moment.... Capture the beauty...... Capture the pureness.......

Niagara Falls

California 2022 as the sun sets over the ocean

<u>CLIMBING THE TREE</u>

As I climbed this tree to get a better look inside. I saw the scars, holes and so much more. This tree has a story to tell. The main story this tree speaks: **I AM STILL STANDING**. Through the hurricanes, tornadoes, and wars. This tree speaks "LIFE". This tree has been through a great deal over the years but the main story I received by looking at his tree and climbing it. No matter what has happened, this tree survived it all! Like Gods love for us.

Spreading the Sunshine as much as possible. Florida 2022

New York City... no place like home.

I have been around the world and loved every moment of it. This time around it is different. Why? Because this time I am going with a clean pair of eyes. I am looking at life differently and trying to see God in everything.

Looking with a different pair of eyes brings so much more clarity in life and how to apply the new clarity to my daily living.

God wants to give you a new pair of eyes to see things differently in your life and what is around you.

Life happens we all have faced something in life that hit us with a major blow to our household. How did you handle that blow? How are you handling what is thrown at you? With God when things come our way, we have someone who has our back.

Growth

<u>GROWTH</u>
<u>STARTING FROM THE BEGINNING</u>

Beginning: the point in time or space at which something starts. It is ok to start over. It is ok to learn new things and apply them to your daily living. Never be afraid to start over! Never be afraid to learn new things. Always be open to learn and grow. It starts off small and can grow into greatness. Apply everything to making your life better.

<u>**Growth**</u>: the process of increasing in physical size or something that has grown or is growing.

God wants you to trust the process in all aspects of your life. It may look small now but keep the process and focus on HIM and watch it grow. Remember that mustard seed.

<u>Matthew 13:32</u>- Though it is the smallest of all seeds, yet when it grows, it is the largest of garden plants and becomes a tree, so that the birds come and perch in its branches.

Miami, Florida

Mexico

<u>MOTHER NATURE</u>

When you are stranded in the wilderness, you can use nature to create shelter to survive the wilderness.
Look at the photo before. Using sticks, mud and leaves can help create a hut (shelter).
God has created everything we need to survive before technology was created.
It is time to get back to our roots and learn how to survive off the land again.

Florida

Massachusetts - Whale Watching

<u>WHALES</u>

God is so amazing. So, the story behind this photo will blow your mind. We are out deep in the sea and no animals in site. I start to pray asking God to bring the dolphins and whales around. Next thing I hear God say look to your right. This whale was waving at us. The captain turns the boat in the direction and then we see dolphins and whales swimming and creating a show for us. The amazing creatures God have created. Just beautiful.

The Butterfly

<u>BUTTERFLY</u>

The caterpillar has to go through stages before it can become a beautiful butterfly. The amazing transformation is a process.

Let us now apply this to our daily lives. The life changing moments you go through in life. Once you have been transformed fully and complete you then become the Butterfly.

The sky is the limit for greatness. Now the process is not easy, but it is well worth it. Be great and spread your wings and fly.

Looking down at the land from the plane.

The depths of the sea and shades of the water. Beautiful

Different layers in the sky
Breath Taking Moments
Capture the Essence
Pay close attention to God's creations
Embrace the beauty
Take time out and cherish nature
Take a break and relax

Circle formation in the sky. Look deeper into the sky.

Buffalo Sunrise
March 30, 2022

<u>Colors and The Meanings</u>

<u>Red:</u> energy, action, confidence, courage, change, passion and strength

<u>Blue:</u> open space, freedom, imagination, inspiration, intuition, faith, trust, loyalty, confidence and healing

Purple: Royalty

White: Purity, cleanliness and peacefulness

Silver: hope, meditation, mystic visions tenderness, unconditional love, spiritual gifts

Green: healing, energy, freshness, growth harmony and nature

Brown: Compassion, comforting, fertility, earth, natural, wholesome, peace and nurturing

PAINTING THE SKY

Waking up to the sunrising and the beautiful colors God paints the sky with. Just amazing on how the sun can create the essence that can make you stop what you are doing and enjoy the beautiful sight.

Lake George

<u>THE PROCESS</u>

The action or process of bringing something into existence. The bringing into of existence of the universe, especially when regarded as the act of GOD. GODS handy work....

<u>My Request For The Readers:</u>

Please take time out and enjoy your life. You only have one life to live. Please take time out and look around. Embrace life and Gods creation. Live your life to the fullest and make sure you capture the moment.

I pray this blessed you.

Remember Gods hands are moving and if we take the time to pay attention, we won't miss it.

<u>G.O.D.S</u>
<u>P.R.O.P.E.R.T.Y</u>

G- Glorifying Him
O- Obedience
D- Deliverance
S- Salvation

P- Power
R- Rejoice
O- Only One
P- Praising Him
E- Eternity
R- Resurrection
T- Trusting Him
Y- Yearning for Him

I cannot say I am perfect because there is only one perfect being and that is GOD. I can say now that I know HIM for myself and have a personal relationship with the my Heavenly Father/ABBA/Yahweh.

I will always praise him, worship him, be obedient to GOD and Accountable to God. This book is to help open your eyes to see deeper and more clearly of Gods mighty handy works. Do not miss what HE is doing in the spiritual realm as well in the physical. GOD is speaking in so many ways and HE wants to get our attention.

<u>**Assignment**</u>

I want you to start taking 1 day for yourself and rest. Take time out to recharge your spirit and rest your mind. I want you to start loving on yourself more each day. Take time out and go for a walk, ride a bike, read a good book, stay in bed. Whatever it is... take time out for you. Treat yourself because you deserve it.

THE BEGINNING LOGO

THE COMPLETION

www.godsproperty2022.com